RUSSELL PUBLIC LIBRARY

S0-ADP-568

Welsbacher

Iowa

32710

C-
977.7
Wy

DATE DUE

1998	

DISCARDED

PRINTED IN U.S.A.

RUSSELL PUBLIC LIBRARY
32710

C-
977.7
Wy

The United States

Iowa

Anne Welsbacher
ABDO & Daughters

visit us at
www.abdopub.com

Published by Abdo & Daughters, 4940 Viking Drive, Suite 622, Edina, Minnesota 55435.
Copyright © 1998 by Abdo Consulting Group, Inc., Pentagon Tower, P.O. Box 36036, Minneapolis, Minnesota 55435 USA. International copyrights reserved in all countries. No part of this book may be reproduced in any form without written permission from the publisher.

Printed in the United States.

Cover and Interior Photo credits: Archive Photos, Corbis-Bettman, Peter Arnold, Inc., SuperStock

Edited by Lori Kinstad Pupeza
Contributing editor Brooke Henderson
Special thanks to our Checkerboard Kids—Raymond Sherman, Gracie Hansen, Brandon Isakson, Priscilla Cáceres

All statistics taken from the 1990 census; The Rand McNally Discovery Atlas of The United States. Other sources: *Iowa*, by Fradin and Fradin, Children's Press, Chicago, 1994; America Online, Compton's Living Encyclopedia, 1997; World Book Encyclopedia; 1990.

Library of Congress Cataloging-in-Publication Data

Welsbacher, Anne, 1955-
    Iowa / by Anne Welsbacher.
    p. cm. -- (The United States)
    Includes index.
    Summary: Surveys the people, geography, and history of the state known both as the Corn State and the Black Hawk State.
    ISBN 1-56239-872-5
    1. Iowa--Juvenile literature. [1. Iowa.] I. Title. II. Series: United States (Series)
    F621.3.W45 1998
    977.7--dc21
                                   97-14795
                                   CIP
                                   AC

Contents

Welcome to Iowa

Iowa is called the Hawkeye State. It is named after Black Hawk. Black Hawk was a famous chief of the Sauk nation.

Iowa is also called the Corn State. It grows more corn than any other state! Iowa has many farms.

People in Iowa like to read! Almost every Iowan can read and write.

Parts of Iowa are flat. These areas make good farmland. But some of Iowa has steep hills. The steepest railroad in the country is in Iowa!

Opposite page: Iowa has fertile farmland.

Fast Facts

IOWA

Capital and largest city
Des Moines (193,187 people)
Area
55,965 square miles
(144,949 sq km)
Population
2,787,424 people
Rank: 30th
Statehood
Dec. 28, 1846
(29th state admitted)
Principal rivers
Des Moines River, Mississippi
River, Missouri River
Highest point
1,670 feet (509 m)
in Osceola County
Motto
Our liberties we prize and our
rights we will maintain.
Song
"The Song of Iowa"
Famous People
James Van Allen, "Buffalo Bill"
Cody, Herbert Hoover, John
Wayne, Grant Wood, Abigail Van
Buren, Ann Landers, Jerry
Mathers

*S*tate Flag

*W*ild Rose

*E*astern
Goldfinch

*O*ak Tree

About Iowa
The Hawkeye State

Detail area

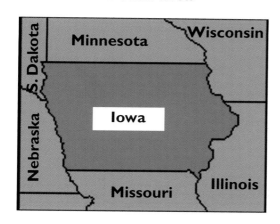

Iowa's abbreviation

Borders: west (Nebraska, South Dakota), north (Minnesota), east (Illinois, Wisconsin), south (Missouri)

Iowa's Treasures

Iowa has very **fertile** soil. Iowa also has lots of water. The weather in Iowa is good for growing **crops**.

In some parts of Iowa, the soil is deep and black. It is great for farming.

In other parts, the soil is not as deep or black. But even this soil is very good for farming. This is why Iowa is such a good farm state!

Iowa is cold in the winter and hot in the summer. It rains year-round. In the winter it also snows.

Opposite page: Iowa's soil is good for growing corn.

Beginnings

The first Iowans lived in the area 12,000 years ago! About 3,000 years ago, they began to build **mounds**. They were called Mound Builders.

A mound looks like a small hill. It is dirt that covers up something. The Mound Builders buried their dead in mounds. They made the mounds in shapes like animals or people.

Early Iowans were Sauks, Fox, and other groups of Native Americans. In the late 1600s, French explorers came. In 1803, the French sold Iowa and other areas to the United States.

Settlers forced many Native Americans to move. Chief Black Hawk and others fought to keep their land. This was the Black Hawk War.

In 1846, Iowa became the 29th state. In the 1860s, the United States fought the Civil War. Southern states wanted slavery. Northern states did not. This is what led to the Civil War. Many Iowans fought for the North.

By 1880, Iowa had many railroad tracks running all over the state. Only four states had more!

In 1920, U.S. women won the right to vote. Iowa women like Carrie Chapman Catt helped win this right.

In the 1930s, there was a bad **drought**. It was a hard time for farmers. Many lost their farms.

In the 1980s, more farmers lost their farms. Today there are still many farmers in Iowa. But more people live in cities.

An express train from the late 1800s.

B.C. to 1800s

The First Iowans

 10,000 B.C.-1600s: People living in Iowa build hundreds of **mounds**. They are called Mound Builders.

 1690: A trading post is built near Dubuque, Iowa.

 1800s: Settlers from other states move to Iowa. Most of the Native Americans are pushed further west.

Iowa

B.C to 1800s

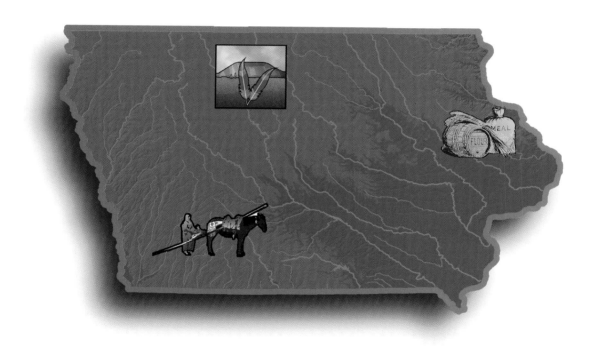

Russell Public Library
1 2 Main St.
P.O. Box 438
Russell, MA 01071
(413) 862-6221

1800s

War Years

1832: Black Hawk and his followers lose the Black Hawk War. They give up their land to white settlers.

1846: Iowa becomes the 29th state.

1860: Both African American and white students attend Grinnell **College**.

1865: The Civil War ends. Iowa soldiers fight on the side of the North.

Iowa
1800s

1907 to Today

Hard Times, New Times

 1907: Fred Maytag, who was born in Iowa, begins making washing machines in Chicago.

 1930s: The Great Depression hits the whole country. Many people have no jobs. **Droughts** hurt farmers even more. Many lose their farms.

 1960s: Winnebago motor homes are **invented** in Forest City, Iowa.

 1990s: Tourism grows as more people visit Iowa.

Iowa
1907 to Today

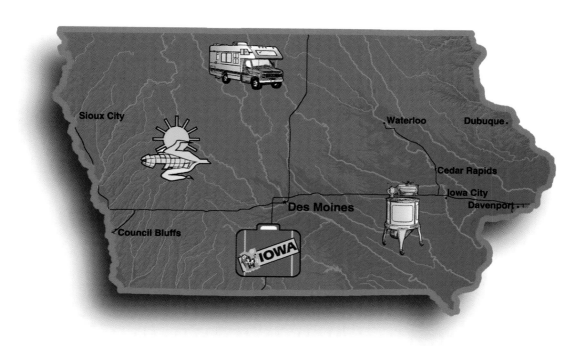

Sioux City

Waterloo   Dubuque.

Cedar Rapids

Iowa City
Davenport.

Des Moines

Council Bluffs

IOWA

Iowa's People

Iowa has 2.7 million people. Many live in **urban** areas.

A lot of Iowans live in **rural** areas. Most people living in Iowa were born in Iowa. Almost no Iowans moved there from other states or countries.

The boy who played The Beaver in the TV show "Leave it to Beaver" was born in Iowa. His name is Jerry Mathers. The man who played Superman on an old TV show also was born in Iowa. His name is George Reeves.

John Wayne, the movie star, was born in Winterset, Iowa. Cloris Leachman was born in Des Moines. She acted in many TV shows and movies.

Charles Ringling was born in Iowa. He and his brothers played circus in their back yard. Later, they made the biggest circus in the country. It is the Ringling Brothers and Barnum and Bailey Circus!

Abigail Van Buren and Ann Landers were born in Sioux City, Iowa. They are twin sisters! They both write newspaper articles.

The artist Grant Wood was born in Iowa. He grew up on a farm. He painted a famous painting. It is called *American Gothic.*

Abigail Van Buren

John Wayne

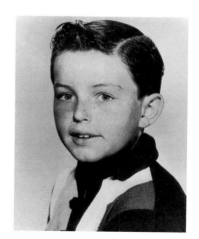
Jerry Mathers

IOWA

Iowa's Cities

Des Moines is the largest city in Iowa. It is also the capital of Iowa. It is near the middle of the state.

Dubuque is in the northeast part of Iowa. It is very pretty. Hills and streams run through the scenic city.

Iowa City and Ames both have a **college**. There are over 13 colleges in Iowa.

Other cities in Iowa are Cedar Rapids, Waterloo, and Davenport.

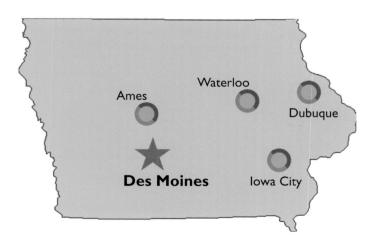

Ames

Waterloo

Dubuque

★
Des Moines

Iowa City

Opposite page: The Iowa State Capitol in Des Moines.

Iowa's Land

Iowa is shaped like a pillow. It is almost square, but not quite! It is near the middle of the United States.

Much of Iowa is flat. But Northeastern Iowa has many hills and streams. It has pine trees and cliffs.

Iowans call the northeast part of Iowa "Switzerland of America." Switzerland is a country in Europe with mountains.

There are many lakes in Iowa. The larger lakes are in the north. Some have high **bluffs**.

The longest river in Iowa is the Des Moines river. It runs down the middle of the whole state! The Missouri River runs along the western **border** of Iowa. The Mississippi River is on the eastern border of Iowa.

To the north of Iowa is Minnesota. To the east are Wisconsin and Illinois. To the south is Missouri. To the west are Nebraska and South Dakota.

Iowa has many trees like elm, hickory, oak, cottonwood, and willow. Flowers like violets, prairie lilies, wild roses, and sunflowers grow throughout Iowa prairies and forests.

Iowa has many white-tailed deer, cottontail rabbits, and foxes. Quails and partridges also live there. Many geese and ducks fly over Iowa on their way south for the winter.

The Mississippi River running through McGregor, Iowa.

IOWA

Iowa at Play

The Iowa State Fair is one of the biggest in the United States. It is one of Iowa's best-loved events. This is because Iowa is such a large farming state.

There is a "living history" farm in Iowa. It shows how farms worked long ago. And it shows how a farm in the future might work.

Iowa has state parks where people can fish, hike, and camp. It has caves to explore.

Every spring in Des Moines there is a boys' and girls' basketball **tournament**. The winners of the tournament are the winners for the year.

Opposite page: Fishing is a fun pastime in Iowa.

Iowa at Work

Many Iowans work on farms. Most farmers grow corn more than any other **crop**. Iowa grows more corn than any state in the United States.

But Iowans have other jobs, too. A lot of Iowans are in sales. They sell **products** to people.

Manufacturing is a big **industry** in Iowa. People in Waterloo make John Deere farm machinery.

School is also important work in Iowa. Many Iowans teach or work in **colleges**. Others teach in public schools.

Opposite page:
A lot of corn is
grown in Iowa.

27

Fun Facts

- The steepest and shortest railroad is in Dubuque, Iowa. It goes up 189 feet (58 m) but is only 296 feet (90 m) long.
- In 1901, it was 100 degrees F (38 degrees C) or hotter in Iowa for 19 days in a row.
- In the late 1800s, a writer named Amelia Jenks Bloomer wore baggy pants. They made it easier for her to move. The pants were named "bloomers" after her.
- A cow named Fawn in Davenport, Iowa, lived through two tornadoes unhurt. In 1962, a tornado carried her through the air. Again in 1967, a tornado blew Fawn through the air. Both times she was not hurt. Fawn was called The Flying Cow.
- Grinnell **College** was started by a man who moved to Iowa from New York City. He moved there after he was told to "Go west, young man!" by a famous newspaper editor.

- Winnebago motor homes were **invented** by John Hanson in the 1960s. He built them in Forest City.
- The movie *Field of Dreams* was made in Iowa. The book and movie *The Bridges of Madison County* is about real covered bridges near Winterset, Iowa.

Covered bridges can be seen throughout Iowa.

Glossary

Bluff: a high part of land that rises up next to a lake or river.
Border: an edge or side of something.
College: a school that people can go to after they finish grade school and high school.
Crop: all the corn or soybeans, etc. that the farmer is growing.
Drought: a long period of time when there is no rain.
Fertile: able to make things grow.
Industry: big businesses such as factories or manufacturing.
Invent: to make for the first time.
Manufacturing: to make things by machine in a factory.
Mound: dirt that covers up something; a mound looks like a small hill.
Product: something people buy that is made.
Rural: in or near the country.
Tournament: a big series of games; the winners of a tournament are the winners for the year.
Urban: in or near a city.

Internet Sites

Iowa Information Network
http://www.iowa.net
A resource for non-profit cultural, social service, and educational organizations in the state of Iowa.

Iowa Virtual Tourist
http://www.jeonet.com/tourist
Here is an excellent introduction to Iowa's geology and geography.

These sites are subject to change. Go to your favorite search engine and type in Iowa for more sites.

PASS IT ON

Tell Others Something Special About Your State
To educate readers around the country, pass on interesting tips, places to see, history, and little unknown facts about the state you live in. We want to hear from you!
To get posted on ABDO & Daughters website
E-mail us at "mystate@abdopub.com"

Index

RUSSELL PUBLIC LIBRARY